Don't miss these exciting Christmas stories, too, by James Bixby!!!

"Old Dingledorf Square", a collection of Christmas stories for the whole family in verse, published by IUNIVERSE.

Christian in tone, relaying good morals and virtues, and told in delightful verse and meter, these old-fasioned Christmas poems will be enjoyed by the whole family!

"Old Dingledorf Square" is a Christmas allegory set in Victorian times that has enormous relevance to today's modern audience. What happens to this little town, famed around the world for their handmade Christmas bells, when a deafening silence overtakes the Christmas joy? Why have the residents lost their religious faith? Come and see how Terwilliger Mugs, a beggar seeking a hot meal and respite from the bitterly cold night, teaches the townsfolk the true meaning of Christmas.

"Cruthers Smuthers and the Green Ghost of Christmas" studies the materialistic theme with a young tyke who becomes the consummate brat through his greedy consumption of Christmas -- until he meets a green ghost that scares him to his wits end!

"The Light of the Beggar" focuses on two urban beggars who view their lack of wealth differently-- one with derision, the other, with Christlike optimism.

These allegorical and spiritual poems will captivate the mind through sonorous and memorable rhyme set to match the music of Christmas.

Chuck Salty, a physician and illustrator par-excellence, will delight your eyes with fanciful characters from the innocence of childhood.

James F. Bixby holds two degrees in classical languages and has taught in both elementary; and secondary education. He has spent most of his life in Michigan, where he still lives today.

The Mystery of "The Christmas Dollhouse"

James F. Bixby

Photographs by:

Michael H. Powers

iUniverse, Inc.
New York   Bloomington

The Mystery of "The Christmas Dollhouse"

iUniverse books may be ordered through booksellers or by contacting:

iUniverse
1663 Liberty Drive
Bloomington, IN 47403
www.iuniverse.com
1-800-Authors (1-800-288-4677)

Because of the dynamic nature of the Internet, any Web addresses or links contained in this book may have changed since publication and may no longer be valid. The views expressed in this work are solely those of the author and do not necessarily reflect the views of the publisher, and the publisher hereby disclaims any responsibility for them.

ISBN: 978-1-4401-7141-3 (sc)
ISBN: 978-1-4401-7142-0 (ebk)

Printed in the United States of America

iUniverse rev. date: 8/19/2010

Introduction

"The Mystery of the Christmas Dollhouse" will bring joy to your life, as you turn the pages to learn the true meaning of Christmas from a little girl's heart. Because she is lost, lonely, and disoriented from being an orphan, Melanie's Aunt Ruth and Uncle Emil take her into their home for her first Christmas apart from her parents. From Emil and Ruth Wassel, Melanie comes to experience a Christmas like none she has ever before imagined for the cheerfulness and spirit of the Yuletide live in her aunt and uncle's hearts.

Like little children anticipating the arrival of Santa Claus, Emil Wassel and his wife Ruth rejoiced over every detail of preparing for this great feast of Christmas, especially for this Christmas of 1956 when their little niece Melanie came to live with them. In fact, few Christmas castles, anywhere, could boast of a greater festive and gay mood for the holidays than Emil and Ruth Wassels' domicile, for they scrimped on not one of the trappings of Christmas cheer, no matter how minuscule.

Emil Wassel devoted himself all year long to planning for everything that could make a spirit jolly, from the top of his Christmas castle to its very bottom. Likewise, few spirits were so merry as Ruth Wassels' in preparing those delightful holiday treats that help to make one's heart sing and dance with the sugar plum fairies. Such a joy the Christmas holidays were to Emil and Ruth Wassel every year, but this year was particularly special for the prospect of raising Emil's brother's daughter, Melanie, would now make them, a childless couple, parents.

Nevertheless, in spite of all the holiday merriment, there was something missing in the home where Melanie came to live with her aunt and uncle at Christmastime. Something mysterious and unpredictable, and as inscrutable as the Incarnation of God Himself become Man, surrounded this little orphaned girl who, too, kept Christmas in her own idiosyncratic way.

If you turn the pages of this old-fashioned Christmas story about family, hearth, and home, you will come to realize that there is something much larger than one's own expectations about the feast of Christmas that raises every heart each year to something more wonderful, unpredictable and sacred about the greatest of all human events, the Birth of God's Son. As one matures in the Christian faith, the Birth of God's Son gains more meaning and something new and different and more uplifting is captured each Christmas Season. It is hoped that "The Christmas Dollhouse" may add something, however small, to the philosophical truth that Christmas is a feast of children, for children, and about children, no matter how old or young they may be. God bless and Merry Christmas to all who turn these pages!

Forward

Michael Powers is especially to be thanked for his skilled photography in rendering an adroit pictorial peek into the fictitious world of "The Mystery of the Christmas Dollhouse." As one views the attractive rendering of this book cover, there looms a story in itself which yearns to be told concerning this toy "about which all little girls dream."

The dollhouse, a family heirloom, was resurrected from obscurity in an upper attic recess and then repainted with a fresh coat of new acrylics by young Elizabeth Rochon under the schooled artistic counsel of her mother Marci Rochon and her father Jerry Rochon, both professional artists and dear friends. The admixture of authentic color combinations allowable for such Queen Anne style Victorian dwellings of the 1800's was trustworthily preserved in the final pictorial painting of the Christmas Dollhouse by the dutiful research and high tech production of the Rochon clan.

It was only after many persevering 'takes' by Michael Powers, a truly aesthetically conscientious artist and scientific precisionist in photography that the perfect angle, most correct light exposure, and vivacious expressions could be captured on the faces of the little starlets of the "Christmas Dollhouse." In search of just the right subjects to pose for Melanie Wassel, a nine year old and protagonist in "The Christmas Dollhouse" story, and her nine year old companion and cousin Karen Winters, two up-and-coming child stars, most definitely, could not be ignored by virtue of their sheer excellence, even though by happenstance they were both Michael Powers and Genvieve Powers own offspring. It should be noted that these worthy candidates were interviewed, screen-tested, costumed, and made-up by their own mother, Genvieve Powers, who recommended them highly because they were graduates of her own academically competitive home-school.

Finally, the furnishings and splendid internal decor of "The Christmas Dollhouse" interior was tastefully undertaken by Genvieve Powers and completed by her with the true plumb and finesse that such "painted lady" homes of the glorious Victorian era of the 1800's deserved. No delicate detail of wall coverings, drapes, rugs, tablecloths, pictures, tableware and even tea ware was overlooked in the creative process by the astute taste and predilections of Genvieve Powers.

A multitude of thanks and blessings is wished every Christmas to the entire Powers clan for their kind generosity in performing a plethora of chores and errands, so necessary for the successful termination of such a creation as "The Christmas Dollhouse." Final accolades and thanks must go, in conclusion, to sweet Gracie Powers, Brendan, Bridget, Mary Clare and Noelle.

To Tom Ulrich, a great Catholic friend, thanks for all of your detailed and strategic computer savvy!

Contents

To My Dear Wife Ruth Ann

and to

Our Lady Of Good Books

Always My Inspiration!

I. The Preparation

The spirit of Christmas cheer glowed warmly through the hearth and home of Emil Wassel when his little niece Melanie came to live with him. Like a string of Christmas lights his wife Ruth reflected all the merriment, too, of Melanie's presence; for she and Emil had never been blessed with children through the years the way Emil's brother Ted had been. It was a very sad Christmas the year before when Melanie lost her parents and her baby brother. Ted Wassel, his wife Chris, and their baby Joseph had all departed to their Maker the night after Christmas in a tragic house fire while they were asleep. For some unearthly reason Melanie had been spared along with a few of her belongings; for she was visiting with Emil and Ruth, as she so often had done, due to their fondness for her. Such a bleak Christmas was it when Emil lost his younger brother Ted that he barely resembled his normally jovial self. Emil could not help but review the trauma of Christmas '55 as he drove home from work this Christmas Eve in his old red GM pick-up truck.

The air was frosty and the wind was blowing the snow clouds into position for the arrival of Santa, as Emil struggled up the front steps of his home with a Christmas tree in each arm. The clouds were dark, black, and foreboding, a sight which could make Christmas shoppers pull their scarves tighter and walk more briskly. On the Wassels' front door a gigantic Christmas wreath, fashioned from backyard evergreen cuttings, cheerfully welcomed everyone with its fragrant pine odors. A moment before Emil had dropped several large paper sacks containing paraphernalia from Christmas shopping on the front steps.

Unloading the pick-up was always a chore that exhausted Emil's portly frame. Ruth had been peeking through the muslin curtains of the dining room window in expectation of Emil's arrival, and she promptly opened the front door to greet him as she had done every afternoon for forty some years.

"Emil, put one of those trees down now. You don't need to carry them both in at once!" offered Ruth eagerly.

"Relax, dear, I have them in a bear hug, each one. One at a time, you're right, dear. I promise they won't escape my grasp, Ruthie. Why don't you pick up those bags ahead of me—there on the steps?"

Ruth quickly bent over and snatched up the large brown bags that were nearly as big as she was. It was not the simplest task for her anymore, as she had passed those fruitful middle years of life; furthermore, the door being opened made her uncomfortably cold too.

"I've put the sheets on the floor and the stands are in place just as you wanted, Emil. You can bring those beauties right in here. Where did you buy them? Melanie's just going to be so tickled."

"Ruthie, don't you remember how many years now I have gone over to Fred's filling station for the trees? Say, where's Melanie? She's usually at the door to greet me."

"Oh, she's playing in her room. You know how she's been on edge lately." clarified Ruthie.

"Anyhow, when you see her, darling, tell her I can use some help—I've a special chore for her to do." Emil puffed and squeezed his rotund self through the front door of their Grosse Pointe home with a Christmas tree in tow. His face scintillated with no less excitement than the jolly old man of the North who journeys across the skies each Christmas Eve. Then he hauled indoors the second tree.

"There." wheezed Emil as he set the trees down on each side of him. "What do you think, my dear?" Nearing the age of retirement, Emil did not have the physical stamina of earlier years; nevertheless, his Christmas spirit was undaunted. He paused momentarily with a full green fir balanced on each side of him in the middle of the living room floor.

"Two trees this year? It's just too much for you, Emil," commented Ruth Wassel.

"Now we can have one in both of the big front windows. Besides, one of the trees is going to be for Ted's family from now on, especially after that terrible fire last Christmas. You know how we're obliged to celebrate more merrily this year for Melanie since it's her first Christmas with us. Did Fred ever give me a couple of real gems, darling!" said Emil with great pride. "Do you really like them, Ruthie?"

"They truly are the most beautiful trees I've ever seen, Emil," returned Ruthie as she closed the front door with vigor and smiled warmly. "I'm sure Melanie will just be beside herself!" said Ruth Wassel merrily.

"Only trouble was it took me so long to decide whether to buy the scotch pines or the Douglas firs. Of course, we've always had firs so I finally decided tradition would win again. Then I debated over which fir trees looked the fullest and the greenest," explained Emil.

Ruth Wassel at once took Emil's wraps after he had rested the two trees up against the living room fireplace; therefore, very little of the Wassels' mantel was visible with all of its decorative Christmas bric-a-brac. Every year Emil and Ruth would nostalgically arrange across the top of the mantel the cute little candled figures of cherubic angels and a motley group of Dickensian characters, all smiling with their ruddy cheeks. Then they would painstakingly drape the front with freshly cut evergreen. At each end there always stood a prize poinsettia plant with clusters of ivy hugging the bases.

Like the bellows for a furnace Emil puffed and puffed into his cupped hands several times, alternating this with rubbing his thick palms back and forth, as he enjoyed being indoors, cozy and safe from the winter weather. In her hands Ruth held Emil's cranberry smoking jacket for him that perfectly matched his cranberry bow tie which glowed with holiday fervor against his white shirt like Santa's cheeks above his white beard. "It's really cold out there and it's clear we're going to have some kind of a fierce snow storm," said Emil emphatically. "Take a look out the front window and see those dark snow clouds forming in the North. Why it'll be a blizzard, the way it looks. There's nothing quite like a white Christmas though. I just wouldn't feel right without it," explained Emil.

"If we don't have one, it won't be because you lack any Christmas spirit," replied Ruth jovially.

Straightway Emil and Ruth scurried about their chores as though they thought something of the season's cheer would escape them if they did not hurry. Emil wrestled with one of the stately firs until it rested snugly within its tree stand in front of the large living room window of mullioned glass. Then the second tree was raised before the dining room window, thus making the front of the Wassels' red brick colonial a virtual display of Yuletide green. Although many of the homes in this section of Grosse Pointe Farms looked much like the Wassels' home all year long, constructed of red brick after the war, there was something especially unique about the Wassels' domicile at Christmas time.

While Emil and Ruth planned their work all year long, it was not until two weeks before Christmas that the spectacular decor of their Christmas castle began to materialize, first on the outside and finally on the inside. From the street, the passers-by could only marvel at the multi-colored lights which bedecked each and every evergreen in the front yard. Santa's helper had also bordered his windows with those special blinking lights which gleefully danced in the darkness once they were lit. The front lawn was populated with illuminated Christmas dolls of all kinds: dancing reindeer and pixie elves, fat snowmen in top hats, lovers hugging in sleighs, kilted skaters in pairs, cranberry-cheeked carolers with sheet music, excited skiers in long stocking caps, and giggling shoppers with armfuls of bulging bags. It tickled the Wassels to see the people pause on a Christmas Eve to glut their eyes in the incandescent sculptures of Emil and Ruth's work. And how they both inwardly glowed because their niece Melanie was also here with them this Christmas; therefore she too could enjoy all the mirth of this splendorous holiday decor along with them. Children stopped and stared in wonderment, giggling and laughing with holiday merriment. Lovers huggled and snuggled up if they happened to pass by in their cars and they always came around the block a second time to tarry.

Nobody could ignore the magical merriment of the Wassels' home, and it was no wonder, for Emil added a new creation of Christmas decor each year to the exterior of his Christmas castle. This Christmas, most of all, was to be particularly joyous. This year it pleased Emil to affix atop his chimney a pudgy, round Santa Claus which had been fashioned adroitly from a concoction of plastic garbage bags in red and stuffed full of sawdust so they would blow freely in the wind. The head, though, had been molded from a white bag and it grinned with a perma-prest smile etched on its face and so this Santa was strategically positioned in a floodlight placed nearby on the roof. This year the face of this homemade Santa laughed with all of the megalomania of Humpty-Dumpty to the passing spectators who were bundled up in their winter-warm accouterments. It was held down by tie ropes, and it blew gently back and forth in the north wind from its roof perch.   Emil had done everything possible to put nighttime strollers in the festive gay mood of the season. From all over the Grosse Pointe area cars lined up bumper to bumper in the evenings to gawk, to laugh, and to enjoy this flirtatious winter carnival of electrical fun. No detail had been overlooked this year to celebrate in every way the festivities of the Christmas season, for Melanie was to be henceforth a part of the Wassels' Christmas joy ever after. What a joy filled their hearts, what a feeling of cheer on this Christmas Eve of 1956.

While watching her husband's flurry of activity with the trees, Ruth chuckled and her ruddy cheeks bounced with excitement against her fair Germanic complexion as though reddish rubber balls protruded imperceptibly from her face, for she understood fully her husband's fondness for Christmas. If any face dispelled the corpulence of Christmas time, it was indeed Ruth Wassels'. Once the trees were safely in their stands, Ruth exited to prepare the freshly cooked delights of their Christmas feast and to look for their niece Melanie.

Delighting in his work, Emil nervously meandered back and forth from the dining room to the living room, pondering such minutiae as where each bulb and strand of tinsel would go on the two trees. How quickly the Wassels' living room and dining room had inhaled that pungent evergreen odor which smelled so delicious you almost wanted to taste it.

In order to check on her husband's doings, Ruth then entered the living room again in her bright red dress, which was trimmed at the neck and sleeves with fine white lace. She was tying about her waist as she walked a gala-colored Christmas apron that was embroidered with a sleigh scene from Currier and Ives. Emil was standing before the tree and holding his chin rather pensively. With beautiful dreams of decorated trees, Emil plotted and planned his work.

"What do you think of the trees in those positions, Ruthie? Are their best sides showing?" asked Emil.

"I just love them, Emil," returned Ruth. "I hoped you would," said Emil ecstatically.

He walked over to Ruth, who was in the doorway, and planted an enthusiastic Christmas kiss on her right cheek. Overhead the mistletoe acknowledged their love and the Christmas cards around the doorway blew so delicately opened and closed as they all wished Emil and Ruth a hearty "Merry Christmas" with the silent whisper of their breaths.

"Are you working on the Christmas dinner yet?" queried Emil.

"Of course. I promise it's going to be my very best! And there's a heap of food to prepare for tonight's meal with your sister Jeniffer coming over and that starving husband of hers."

"Ken isn't a bad fellow." said Emil. "He really knows how to celebrate the holidays with a big meal. And that's what we all truly need this year," confirmed Emil. "He's simply a bundle of fun."

"He sure knows how to eat," returned Ruth. "Anyway I've got to hurry and prepare the stuffing, the turkey, and all the trimmings or there'll be nothing for them," clarified Ruth Wassel.

"By the way did you tell Melanie to come and help me, Ruthie? I have something very special for her to do. What's she been doing now that she's out of school for vacation?" wondered Emil.

"Yes, I told her, Emil. Hasn't she come out to help you yet?" clarified Ruth with arms akimbo. "All she seems to want to do lately is play in her room with that dollhouse of hers. Remember the one Teddy made for her a couple of Christmases before the fire?"

"Oh yes, I know the dollhouse you mean. Just remember, darling, to tell her I've got something very special for her to do," stated Emil.

In the meantime Emil had made several trips to the attic for the Christmas tree ornaments and he was stacking the boxes before the hearth just as painstakingly as Santa would while going about his merry chores on Christmas Eve. Squatting before the fireplace, Emil worked assiduously for a time with the ornaments, lining them up and checking that none had been damaged or misplaced. After a time, he was taken aback by the appearance of Melanie beneath the verdant evergreen branches of the Christmas tree towering above her. Unbeknownst to Emil, she had been idling there for several minutes, fingering the hem of her soft velvety cranberry dress. Ruth had recently sewn it so this new daughter of hers would reflect all the cheerfulness of the season, for the borders of her Christmas dress had been embellished with tiny red berries and laced leaves of ivy. Long brown hair fell down upon Melanie's back, draping slightly over her shoulders. Her hair, straight and simple in style, glistened and shone in the vanishing light that foreshadowed the arrival of the snowstorm. A blank distant look possessed her frail features while she stared up at the Christmas tree as if she were frozen.

Her bright blue eyes dominated her countenance, because they were so big and so round, exactly like her moon-shaped face. In spite of the twinkle to her eyes, there was an emaciated look to her whole countenance—like that of a child who has just recovered from a severe bout of influenza. Yet, Melanie was so captivating in her pathetic isolation before the Christmas tree that she reminded one of a teddy bear that was yearning to be picked up and hugged.

Even though Melanie persisted in her aloofness before the living room fir tree, now fingering the tips of the branches with her fingers, Emil fumbled with the boxes of decorations until they were all placed just so beneath the fireplace: the strings of lights and the endless assortment of hypnotically entrancing tree hangers.

Momentarily, Emil and Melanie were worlds apart; one on the floor playing with the decorations and the other looking upward through the heights to the top of the fir tree. Throughout this interlude, Melanie distracted herself for just a moment or two as she folded over a little note she had placed in an envelope on an evergreen branch, about eye level to her nine year old height.

The note was simply addressed to her new mommy and daddy: "Are we going to St. Anthony's for Christmas?" She wanted so much for her uncle Emil and Aunt Ruth to receive the Christmas note, yet she was at the same time haltingly reluctant.

"Do you like the fir trees, Melanie?" asked Emil excitedly.

"Look. It's snowing outside, Uncle Emil," announced Melanie with joy.

Thereupon she scampered at once to the only other window in the living room, the one without the tree in front of it. Ordinarily Melanie was quite at ease with Emil and Ruth, and so she felt rather free to do as she pleased. She looked upon them as grandparents in a way because Emil and Ruth were so much older than her own parents.

"I see, but don't you want to help me decorate the Christmas trees, Melanie?" requested Emil with a certain frustration to his voice over her evasiveness.

Perseveringly, an entranced Melanie gazed out the window at the falling flakes of snow, which confirmed the artfulness of nature's own seasonal showmanship. Both Emil and Melanie continued in their pastimes for some time, until both Christmas trees were fully covered with ornaments and the ground was blanketed in snow. Throughout the whole decorating ritual and while watching all the flakes of snow delicately falling to the ground, Melanie slipped away from before the front of the living room window but once, only to rethink her little gift and to readjust the white enveloped Christmas card which she had made and placed there on just the right fir branch at eye level. It was merely token recognition that each gave to the other, for every once in awhile Melanie would glance uncertainly at the tree while Emil glimpsed at Melanie kneeling before the living room window.

As Emil continued his absorbing decorative duties and endeavors before the fir trees in both of the front rooms, the living room and dining room respectively, a faint humming, barely audible, could be heard in the air, for it was a celestial sound as soft and mellow as the voice of an angel and as light as the snow floating down beyond the living room window. This pleasant music escaped Emil who poured his whole heart and soul into the ornamental chores at hand. One after the other a melancholic procession of notes followed as the melody of "Silent Night, Holy Night" whispered its way heavenward. As long as Emil enjoyed the merry task of trimming the trees, this mournful music from a soprano voice caroled forth a sadness of the heart in accompaniment to the congregation of snowflakes accumulating outside the snow-covered windows.

Having completed his frolicsome tasks with the empty ornament boxes all stacked neatly before the hearth once again, Emil stood back and indulged his eyes in the tinseled beauty of the bulbs, lights, and tree. Unable to contain the rush of jovial cheer in his heart any longer, Emil Wassel spun his corpulent self around to look for Melanie, but mysteriously she had vanished. Consequently, Emil removed all the boxes to the attic, cleaned up the scattered pine needles from the rug and finally trailed the succulent scents of roasting turkey out into the kitchen, the culinary retreat of Ruth Wassel. When Emil poked his head around the kitchen door, Ruth was carefully removing from the oven a tray of sweetly scented molasses sugar cookies shaped like Santa, his reindeer, and sleighs. Ogle-eyed Emil pranced up to the table where Ruth was unloading the treats into the cookie jar so he could sneak a preview. It pleased Emil to move as close as possible in order to sample their excellence in some surreptitious way. Standing behind Ruth with his head leaning over her shoulder as unobtrusively as possible, Emil swung a hungry arm around her waist to capture his prey.

"Now, Emil, you needn't try to eat everything up before the arrival of the company," remonstrated Ruth Wassel a little impatiently.

"I only want to test their incredible taste, sweetheart," retorted Emil. His mouth was not only stuffed with the cookie he had snatched but also with his words, for which there was then precious little space; hence, his reply was a rather incoherent mishmash.

Exposed to Emil's idiosyncrasies for years, Ruth Wassel had grown immune to his mischievous ways. Looking up from her work, she said: "Have you finished decorating the trees yet, dear?"

"As sure as Christmas Eve is the Night Before Christmas," responded Emil most confidently. "You have to come and inspect my work– right away. It looks really great, Ruthie!" Holding another molasses cookie between his teeth, Emil pulled and pulled at Ruth's arm even though she had not quite finished with her culinary pursuits.

"I'll bet they're exquisite," stated Ruth ecstatically. With her spatula she dropped the last few cookies from the tray into the jar and then she followed her husband excitedly into the dining room. Ruth stood there like an astonished school girl with her eyes glued to the splendorous beauty of Emil's efforts." Why the fir tree looks bigger and fancier than it did last year, honey," vibrated Ruth.

Before Emil could respond, his wife had hurried into the living room to study the delightful display of decorations that dressed the other Christmas tree. As her eyes scanned the utter beauty of this Christmas tree in the living room and the delightful glory of the tinseled, ornamental wonderland of figurines, glass bulbs, and electrical lights, so boldly displayed in a veritable rainbow of seasonal colors of red and green, she failed to see the ever so tiny Christmas card from her new daughter Melanie. The card was no bigger than a nine year old child's diminutive hand, and it rested so modestly upon one of the lower branches, set slightly back from the front of the stately fir. Nor had Emil noticed this childish alteration in his so inimitably perfect yuletide trimming efforts because Melanie had slipped her little handmade Christmas card onto its tree branch perch earlier, at a most clandestine moment, when he would not notice what she was doing. And how inconspicuous it was in the sea of ornamental beauty that surrounded it.

"Why I don't remember when Christmas ever seemed more marvelous," beamed Ruth from one side of her face to the other.

More quickly than shoppers scurrying from one store to the other for last minute Christmas shopping, Emil flitted from Ruth's presence to the front vestibule closet for the large sacks of gifts which Ruth had earlier secured there. Through all the hustle and bustle, Emil still could converse with his wife while lugging the bags of goodies.

"I can't believe how cheerful things are with Melanie here and all this celebrating and decorating," Emil laughed.

"It will be such a delight this year, sweetheart, I am sure." beamed Ruth Wassel. "So we've finally come to one of my favorite parts of Christmas, wrapping the gifts," said Ruth happily. "Let me see first what you have for Melanie from the store; I'm so excited."

"This is no ordinary gift. I thought and thought about what to give her. I liked our idea of a doll the best, and so I put this one together from parts lying around the toy shop," explained Emil.

"It's unlike any other doll you've ever seen in my toy store. We have to be careful, though, in case she comes in here unexpectedly, Ruthie," admonished Emil somewhat nervously who was on the floor, fumbling through a large sack. Ruth had joined him too on the floor in her great anticipation. "You had better take a good look and see, if by any chance, she's nearby, Ruthie," directed Emil.

"Where did she go? I thought she was in here helping you decorate the trees?" queried Ruth. As she stood up, she had to lean on a nearby rocking chair to steady herself. After she stood erect, Ruth dropped her hands into her apron pockets to rest them.

"She didn't want to help." clarified Emil. "She looked out the side window for awhile at the snow piling up and then before I knew it, she had vanished."

"I believe Christmas is upsetting her. Let me go and see if she's in her room," counseled Ruth Wassel. Emil fidgeted and fumbled over his bag of goodies while Ruth made a rather quick exit and returned with an expression of pleasant surprise.

"Hurry up, Emil! But do be quiet. Melanie' s fallen asleep and you won't believe how angelic she looks," explained Ruth.

With alacrity, Emil pursued the lead of his wife to the doorway of Melanie's bedroom. There lying on the oval braided, dark blue rug was their new daughter fast asleep with her head cradled in her nine-year-old arm. Her face was turned toward her dollhouse in a state of utter restfulness and peace. The wooden dollhouse, about three feet high, looked protectively over the sleeping Melanie.

This toy, about which all little girls dream, was a masterpiece of the intricacies of carpentry in the miniature, which Melanie's father Ted had built two Christmases before the fire. The entire front of the house was crafted as a most elegantly detailed Victorian style dollhouse that bloomed forth like a veritable Christmas tree with such a rich profusion of colorful shapes and forms that it literally glowed to all onlookers so merrily, reflecting the true spriteliness of the Yuletide season.

Everywhere Melanie's dollhouse broadcasted this unique visual delight of a Christmas tree: a large red cedar shingled roof of three gables, green encasement windows expressing the finest delicacy in elegant leaded glass treatments, white festooned exterior trim decorating the eaves and upstairs and downstairs porches, and lastly the entire clapboard exterior of the house painted richly in brightest royal blue. And if this panorama of scintillating color was not able to dazzle one's eyes exactly like the strings of multi-colored electronic illumination on a Christmas tree then the very fine ornamentation everywhere else would certainly mesmerize one's visual fancies. Consider only the kaleidoscope of sundry shapes and forms of red, yellow, blue and green ornamentation appearing on the fascia board peaks as well as the variegated light rays reflecting from all the tiny window pane shapes of leaded glass. No less amazing to the eyes was the very facade itself of the Christmas dollhouse which stood like a veritable Christmas tree, so lofty with its dominating front tower, that pointed to the sky as a unified whole by coordinating all lesser shapes and forms of the dollhouse exterior into a single fir tree design.

If puerile fascination or Yuletide gratification might not be satisfied by the Christmas tree kind of appearance of Melanie's miniature dollhouse world, one could not ignore, then, the multitude of Lilliputian delights hidden inside the dollhouse itself, which were truly just as ornamental and endlessly variegated as the holiday gifts so artfully arranged beneath a Christmas tree's embrace, allowing no eyes to pass them by with ennui.

Notwithstanding the spirited play that this dream toy could evoke in virtually all little girls at Christmastime, Melanie Wassel was not to be so easily preoccupied or blissfully distracted. In fact she had been concentrating her energies on rearranging the dollhouse's interior— as one might expect most little girls to do with such a toy—but, in a manner having the most salient consequences for herself and her dollhouse world.

Just what was it that Melanie did see, inside this most special of all dollhouses, a miniature world built by the loving hands of her deceased father in a most remarkable way? A brief peek inside this imaginative world of a child at play by her Uncle Emil and Aunt Ruth, standing in the doorway, would have revealed so much, so very, very much. So, indeed, would it to any astute onlooker.

In thus observing, the entire back of this antique wonderland of Victorian architecture had all the traditional rooms open for the playful amusement of the tiny hands of the little lady who would so cherish the arranging of all the delicately carved furniture of elegant mahogany finish; including all such formalities which such stately homes required: a monumental grand piano, dining room table and chairs with accompanying credenza and china cabinet, the bedroom sleigh beds with night stands, the pink cushioned parlor chairs and matching divan, and finally the pot-bellied stove, wash stands, and pantry cabinets for food and sundry other victuals. In fact, no detail had been overlooked by Melanie's father Ted who was a master carpenter and who reveled in expressing his love for his dear daughter with this most special of all gifts that his skills could offer.

Alongside the little home was a junk pile of sorts, including all the miniature playtime paraphernalia common to such dollhouses. There were clothes and jewelry, dishes and silverware, pots and pans—all authentically scaled to the living quarters of the dollhouse. Moreover Melanie had cleared away her fanciest knickknacks including vases, pictures, clocks, heirlooms, pictures, and statuary. In fact, it was a thorough house cleaning which Melanie had undertaken, one which had left none of the house's opulent possessions behind; hence a notable emptiness had overtaken the interior of the little dollhouse. Melanie's father, a skilled carpenter by trade, had hobbied a whole year away in woodcarving; consequently, everything which Ted Wassel had made for his daughter was so perfectly precisioned and scaled to the miniature world of the dollhouse. Even her mother Chris' efforts on the delicate feminine touches had not been overlooked: curtains, rugs, drapes and flowers. In fact, it was a thorough house cleaning which Melanie had undertaken; one which had left virtually nothing behind, save the few plaster doll figurines within; hence a stark bareness had overtaken the interior of the little dollhouse world.

"Should I pick her up, Ruthie, and put her in bed?" asked Emil.

"Oh, no! No, Emil. Leave her be. You might wake her up and I don't want her becoming overtired. There'll be enough excitement this evening." explained Ruth.

Quietly Emil and Ruth light-footed their way back to the living room where they gave themselves fully to the wrapping ritual they so much appreciated and enjoyed. Meanwhile, Melanie dreamed and dreamed about a Christmas she used to know but to which she no longer could return. While Melanie did her dreaming, the endeavors of the adult world materialized into a pile of gifts the likes of which Santa himself would gladly tote around in his enormous sack. Colorful wrapping paper bedecked with old-fashioned Christmas country scenes, ribbon gathered into delightful boughs like flowers in blossom hugged virtually every gift the Wassels wrapped, but no gift received the loving attention that the two paid to Melanie's gift.

Slowly and painstakingly, Emil lifted his treasure from the large paper sack and laid it before Ruth's eager eyes. "Emil, Emil, the doll looks just like Melanie. The sweet demeanor and tender expression is so perfect. A fine job you did in your toy shop! And those wings are just adorable! Why, I just adore the powder blue costume! I'm so sure she'll just love it, too," said Ruth jubilantly.

When the wrapping ended, each gift was then set at the bases of the two trees so attractively that the seasonal covers of popular magazines would cower for shame. Everything to the last item had been so perfectly planned and executed for Christmas Eve by Ruth Wassel. In order to tease the appetites of the guests, tasty hors d' oeuvres had been placed strategically around the room on end tables in elegant crystal servers.

Such delights included a dish of caviar and crackers, a potpourri of carrots, celery, broccoli and cauliflower, a delightful cheese dip, molasses sugar cookies shaped like Santa's elves, home-made chocolate candies formed into Christmas trees, and a fruit basket of dried apricots, fresh apples, oranges and pears. She had time even to light scented pine candles on the mantel and at other key vantage points around the living room and dining room. Emil did his best to make everything just so perfect, too, before the guests arrived; he flipped the switch which flooded the exterior of their Christmas castle in a palette of seasonal color. Having completed their cheerful chores, Emil and Ruth sipped a sample cup of hot buttered rum in their favorite rocking chairs while they chatted for an interval on the sweet inanities to come.

II. The Christmas Party

It was not long that they so entertained one another before the sequential music of the doorbell chimes beckoned them from their rockers to greet the guests. Before you could name Santa's eight reindeer, Emil flew from his seat like a child leaping out of bed on Christmas morning. He swung open the front door with vigor and in stepped his younger sister Jeniffer with her husband Ken and their little girl Karen, but not before a gust of frigid Michigan air and a spray of snow slapped Emil across the cheeks.

"A very Merry Christmas to all of you!" shouted Emil with a merry roll.

"And the very same to you, old boy!" bellowed Ken raucously. Ken threw one of his corpulent arms around Emil's back in a kind of polar bear hug of welcome. In Ken's other arm he had his little girl Karen cradled. She was teeming with much excitement for a nine year old on Christmas Eve, especially because she wanted to give vent to all her holiday expectations as soon as she could free herself from her father Ken's strong arm. Jeniffer, Emil's sister and Ken's wife, was loaded down with two huge sacks of presents.

"Where are the presents to open? Where's the Christmas tree?" squealed Karen who was becoming rather irritated because she was still trapped in her father's huge arm.

After the door was closed and the overcoats, hats, and gloves had been removed, the two families melted into a warm conviviality of Yuletide cheer. The adults relaxed in the nearest easy chair suitable to their comfort and fancy in order to discuss those levities that they most enjoyed on such a festive occasion. With exuberance, Karen skipped merrily about from the Christmas tree in the living room to the one in the dining room.

"They're simply gorgeous!" approved Jeniffer most merrily. "And two of them this year!"

"Can I open a gift? Can I?" begged Karen.

"By the way it's *may* I open a gift, not *can,* Karen. You know better." remonstrated her mother Jeniffer. "Shouldn't we allow the kids to open a gift before dinner?" offered Jeniffer in response.

"Sure. Why not?" supported Emil. "Isn't that what Christmas is all about?"

"Where's Melanie?" wondered Jeniffer.

"Oh! She fell asleep in her room." explained Ruth with hesitation. Although she was a little embarrassed because she had forgotten to wake Melanie before the relatives arrived, her tone of voice tried to hide it as though all was well. "Why don't you go and wake her up, Karen, so you both can open a present before dinner?" suggested Ruth.

Karen, a chubby little girl with a red glow to her cheeks, attired in a plain green dress with a holly design on the sleeves and hem, was quite unaware of what was happening because of her shuffling through the gifts beneath the Christmas tree. "Where's mine? Where's my present?" begged Karen enthusiastically.

"Leave the gifts alone, Karen, and go and wake Melanie as your aunt said," demanded her father Ken. "You are going to make a huge mess. Now hurry up, Karen."

"Ok. Ok," complained Karen vociferously. She strutted from the room in her plain green dress, but her frustration was apparent in the way she shooed her parents away with her hands swinging behind her back as she left the living room.

Once she had entered the back hall to Melanie's bedroom, Emil was up from his Boston rocker to empty the two bags of gifts Jeniffer and Ken had brought. Emil ever so carefully distributed the gifts amongst the others beneath the fir trees, while Ruth left the room momentarily on an errand to the kitchen.

"Wait till you see the surprises we have for you folks," boasted Jeniffer. "I must have spent weeks shopping downtown, looking for just the best thing for each one of you. It's one of the joys of my life, shopping the department stores during the Christmas season: it simply delights me all over, too, and traversing the malls in search of just the right gifts for each one of you. I shiver just thinking of it all! We have something extra special for Melanie, too, this year. How's she been since that terrible ordeal, Emil?"

"She's been kind of aloof, Jeniffer, living in a world all her own. All she ever seems to want to do is play with her dollhouse - you know the one Teddy made for her a couple of Christmases ago," said Emil.

"You certainly remember how it was with them, Emil. Your brother Teddy never had a penny for anything, yet alone enough to buy a stitch for Melanie," continued Ken. "Living out in the sticks, the way they did, there just wasn't enough work for Ted. The big city's where the prosperity is. Besides Melanie's never had a good Christmas, but this year will be different as far as we're concerned. We've spent a small fortune on her and everybody else."

"That's Christmas cheer, Kenny. The real spirit of it all," voiced Emil with zest.

"Who thinks they have Christmas cheer?" inquired Ruth who proudly entered the living room with a tray in her hands. "I can promise you I have more Christmas cheer than anybody else—right here on this tray," bragged Ruth Wassel.

"Does that ever smell like hot buttered rum. And I just love those adorable little holiday cups you have to serve it. Such elegant china!" stated Jeniffer with avid interest.

"You better believe you have more Christmas cheer than anybody!" said Ken, her husband, matter-of-factly.

"Just help yourselves," directed Ruth as she ambled around the living room, serving all the Yuletide revelers. "And if you empty your cups, there's plenty more there in the pitcher."

Once everyone had their cup in hand, Emil offered a holiday toast:

"Cheers to you all. And a Merry, Merry Christmas!" The conviviality spread as the toast was echoed by the spirited tapping of all of the cups.

"It's such a shame we don't have Teddy and Chrissy here the same way we did two years ago. And that cute little baby brother, Joseph, that Melanie had. Things will never be the same," said Jeniffer somewhat melancholically.

"What a tragedy to lose Teddy," affirmed Emil. "I'm just beginning to grapple with it now. He was such a good brother." Emil's eyes were watering and had a glassy look as he carried on with his reminiscences. "Their Christmas, though, was always so frugal—just a tree with a few lights on it and a couple of homemade gifts. But that crib Teddy had carved—what a masterpiece and was he ever proud of it. By the way, those end tables we're using for the appetizers were made by Teddy too. If Chrissy hadn't sewed the way she did, Melanie wouldn't have had a stitch of clothing. They just never knew what a good Christmas was like. Why Teddy worked for people for next to nothing, I'll never know. You simply cannot survive these days that way. There's always been plenty of work around the Pointes and here in Detroit. The U P is copper country, wild forests, and bears; and aside from it being a tourist's paradise for hunting, fishing, and summer vacations, there's very little work to be had. I told Teddy I could find him work in the Grosse Pointes for carpentry, if he would only move down this way, but they loved it up there in the wilderness just eking it out. I guess there really was nothing anyone could do to attract him to the big city. He was simply in love with his sylvan retreat with all its peace and quiet. But no matter how you look at it, Teddy was the best brother in the whole wide world. And I miss him so!"

"You had better believe it. A splendid brother is a perfect description of Teddy," confirmed Jeniffer who was rather agitated from Emil's words. In the meantime, she had refilled her cup and was nervously sipping little mouthfuls of the second serving as she cradled her cup in both hands.

Just then, Karen ambled back into the living room rather distraught with her little pudgy arms akimbo. "Melanie won't come in here. She just sits with her dollhouse and won't come with me," whimpered Karen "She won't let me play with her dollhouse either. Can I open my present now?"

"I'll go and get her, Karen, and then you can open your present," said Ruth reassuringly.

While Ruth was gone, Emil entertained the guests with the fireplace and its ceremonial lighting. Throughout this festivity the anticipation of the children opening the first gifts grew steadily with each log that he placed upon the flaming kindling wood in the hearth. Emil reveled in a euphoric state of cheer as the master of ceremonies, attired in his cranberry smoking jacket, white shirt, and matching cranberry bow tie. He pitched several pinecones and a handful of chestnuts onto the fire for good measure to give the living room that special fragrance and crackling sound that is so familiar on such festive Yuletide occasions. If the Christmas tree lights, the hearth, and the spicy pine candles flickering through the entire living room were not warming enough; then certainly, the hot buttered rum being emptied from the pitcher generated another kind of seasonal warmth. From within and without the Wassels' home was glowing feverishly with cheerfulness when Ruth returned hand in hand with Melanie to the center of this holiday warmth.

"There's my little doll," cheered Emil.

"Is that ever a darling outfit," applauded Jeniffer rather gaily, as she munched on a few freshly dipped chips while she spoke.

"You look just like a darling young lady, Mel," observed Ken who waved approval with his cup.

Little Melanie surveyed the crowded living room and all of its occupants with a bashful reservation. Hesitatingly, she stepped into the center of the excitement and glutted her eyes with a sweeping glance upon the feast of Christmas before her.

"Are all these presents for us?" queried Melanie with a look of surprise.

"They sure are, Melanie - each and every one of them," boasted Emil forthrightly. "And here's a very special one for you, dear," continued Emil as he bent over and fished out an elegantly wrapped gift from beneath the fir tree. The silvery green paper of the gift and the bright blue ribbon of its bow reflected all the Christmas lights in the room and glowed so brightly in its elegant ornamentation. Emil then handed the perfectly square box to Melanie who reluctantly took it in hand.

"There's a special one for you too, Karen," beamed Emil as he struggled to lift upward his rotund frame again after leaning over for the second gift.

Karen quickly made the gift with silvery red paper her own by grabbing it from her Uncle Emil. The bright red silver paper glowed happily to all its admirers in the room with its pert little white bow on top. Thereafter the natural curiosity of being a child on Christmas overwhelmed each of the youngsters as the wrappings were straightway stripped from the two boxes nearly identical in size.

"Wow. Look at what I have. A big Santa Claus," bragged Karen. "He's got a red suit and a hat, and look at the little pair of black boots. Oh, he's really cute."

"So you like what Aunt Ruthie and I gave you for Christmas, Karen?" queried Emil with a festive gay smile all aglow with satisfaction.

"Let me see Melanie's present. What did she get?" interrupted Karen. From her position on the floor, Karen quickly scrambled over in the direction of Melanie.

Meditatively Melanie stared at the doll that she was fondling with her hands. She cold not cope with the thought of such an incredible possession being all her own. Melanie was stunned momentarily from it all, in a kind of blissful state of reverie.

"Do you like it, Melanie?" begged Emil, enthused as an eager little schoolboy.

"Oh, thank you, Uncle Emil. Thank you! Thank you! Is it really mine?" asked Melanie.

"As much as your dollhouse, sweetheart." clarified Emil.

"Oh, thank you. Thank you, Aunt Ruthie!" added Melanie.

"Your very welcome, dear. I hope you enjoy the little doll because it looks like you so much, darling," observed Ruth with such a happy holiday glow.

Oh, I will. I will. I never had a doll like this before. And it's such a pretty angel!" said Melanie with joy.

"Let me see it," challenged Karen who snatched the doll from Melanie. "Aww. I like my Santa doll much more," said Karen as she dropped the doll indifferently into Melanie's lap.

"Now, Karen. We'll have none of that kind of talk," demanded Ken with a furrowed brow.

Melanie simply sat there eyeing her doll in wonderment, as though she were in another world.

"Isn't it about time for dinner, Ruthie?" wondered Emil. "I can smell some mouth-watering turkey and stuffing in the dining room."

"So do I," affirmed Ken zestfully.

"I do believe everything is ready now, so please enter the dining room and take your places around the table," directed Ruth Wassel with a proud smile of warm holiday cheerfulness. "There's a place card for everyone; now do take notice of where Santa wants you to sit!"

As all the Christmastime revelers filed so merrily into the dining room and found their seats, Ruth Wassel looked about the room in utter wonderment as she was about to lay out the serving dishes of this family feast. Something had struck her eyes as being abnormal about the place settings; there were her decorations at each of the places, her green bowed ribbon around each napkin at every place, but there was still something she had not noticed before. Simple little cuttings of evergreen, almost like the pieces left over on the floor when someone brings a fresh fir tree into a home, were lying at every place with a small red ribbon tied around the center of each evergreen sprig. It appeared to be a simple figure of an evergreen cross with the ribbon forming the crossbar. Each decorative red and green Christmas cross was positioned to the right side of each place, next to the spoon. Ruth, thoroughly puzzled, peered quickly around the room for an explanation but could not ascertain the source of this mystery until she eyed her new daughter Melanie sitting so pertly at her seat with a kind of mute, nervous grin on her face. As Melanie too looked around the room to check each one of the places where the relatives sat, she seemed to smile confidently to herself as though all was well. Likewise Ruth Wassel also smiled more happily when she surveyed the guests and her new daughter as she sensed an intimacy burgeoning now between Mother and daughter, for Melanie had creatively added, it appeared, her own touch of Christmas to this ample feast. How this warmed Ruth Wassel's heart.

Moreover, a kind of exhilarating holiday happiness ran through Ruth's heart and soul, a feeling she had never before experienced and it made her want to weep for joy inwardly at its approach. For a moment, she cherished this delightful little discovery as she then began to look with the most loving of eyes upon Melanie while she made her way around the dining table to lay out the treasures of this family feast. Melanie sat there with her eyes downward in a meditative state of apartness with her delicate little hands folded on the lap of her red Christmas dress. Everyone else was so avidly talking and taking in each entree of this Christmas feast as Ruth progressed now with more ardor and enthusiasm as she moved around the table with each serving plate, contemplating and cherishing the joy that was overflowing in her heart.

The snow-puffed potatoes, the buttered orange squash, the sweet red cranberries, the tossed green salad, the spicy sage stuffing, and the waxed beans sat in envious obeisance before the lordly presence of tom turkey. The voracious eyes of all confirmed the scrumptious dexterity of Ruth's work in the kitchen. Rapidly the foods were distributed from the serving plates of white bone china to the eager audience of dishes surrounding. Ceremoniously, Emil, in a state of Christmas euphoria, proceeded to carve the turkey with all the pride of a chef showing off his favorite gourmet dish. Without the slightest hesitation, this congregation of worshipers took their portion and gave homage to the cornucopia, as though their lot was nothing less than the midnight meal that surfeited Santa before his trip abroad. In fact, almost as soon as they were seated, they began to imbibe the victuals of this Christmas dinner, unable to curtail the amplitude of their appetites any longer. Emil made a stop at each of the adult's places to pour a glass of bubbling red wine whose effervescence sent off a spray when poured that tickled one's taste buds. The food traveled from plate to mouth at supersonic speeds, causing the Wassels' dining room to be overtaken by the melody of knives, forks, and spoons tapping out a Christmas overture on the plates.

Melanie, though, only nibbled at her meal and chased the food around her plate with her fork. She was as removed from the festivities at the table as the snow piling up outside the frosted dining room windows on this festive Christmas Eve. Unexpectedly, though, she leapt from her chair at the dining room table and headed toward the double glass doors of mahogany wood at the back of the dining room.

"Where are you going, Melanie?" inquired Ruth

"I have to.... I have to," mumbled Melanie on the run, and in quite an ecstatic hurry.

"Well, all right," interrupted Ruth. "But hurry back, dear, from the lavatory because we have company."

"Ok," returned Melanie who was already through the doorway.

After Melanie had left, Ken Winters refilled his plate with another full course and had nearly devoured the next round as quickly as the first. In girth, Ken Winters was a near perfect duplicate for his brother-in-law Emil. Entering his middle years, Ken showed his age clearly in his bulging mid-section that seriously challenged the amplitude available in his white shirt; furthermore, his thick, round, chubby fingers bespoke of his frequent trips to the refrigerator at midnight. His rotundity was no less remarkable than his tastes; he had a special predilection for the whole turkey dinner being submerged in a bath of sugared cranberries.

Like her husband Ken, Jeniffer Winters was red-faced, plump and pleasant, and truly the perfect compliment to her husband's robust fervor for feasting. Her graying hair, beautifully coiffured in a bouffant, attested to her fashionable nature as there was virtually nothing in vogue of which Jeniffer was unaware. Her crimson colored dress with a subtle snowflake design had an elegant white lace bib. It had been purchased from an expensive Grosse Pointe boutique, was simple in style, and perfectly complimented her premature graying hair. While Emil made his appetite merry with repeated servings of stuffing and gravy, Ruth periodically checked her guests' needs with that schooled glance of the sophisticated hostess. The conversation proved to be just as stimulating as the menu.

"You won't believe the price I paid for my Christmas tree this year, Emil!" bragged Ken Winters.

"Oh yeah?" said Emil with an amused glint in his eyes as he stroked his chin pensively. "Not another one of your stories, Kenny."

"Absolutely! And you won't believe this one either," boasted Ken.

"Well, go ahead. Let's hear it," begged Emil with a curious facetiousness to his voice.

"Well, I was shopping for our Christmas tree a few days ago, going from lot to lot. You know the routine, Emil. After I stopped at two or three lots, I came to this one run by a couple of old-timers. They were nice old gents, but their prices were ridiculously high. Believe it or not, I found this one tree, a real beauty with full branches and a great smell – the best one I saw on all the lots. Would you believe they wanted twenty-five dollars for this scotch pine? I knew it was just what I wanted, though, so I dragged it over to the covered wooden shed where they had the checkout counter. How I love checkout counters and those scatter-brained characters who take forever to ring up your order, especially on a freezing cold December evening, after work. I don't think they can count much past twenty-five. Anyhow, I must have stood there twenty minutes, freezing my can off, and the needles on it were scratching my face and neck because this jerk in line behind me kept pushing into me with his tree. Finally, I couldn't stand it any more, so I figured I'd take it to the car, tie it on, and go pay for it. Guess what? I had Jeniffer's little red car there—that puddle-jumper foreign car. I had one devil of a time tying it on the roof. Once I got it in place on the roof, I looked around and around and there wasn't a soul in sight, so I jumped in and drove off. Besides, it looked like a blizzard was coming; you know the kind of one that just gave us a white Christmas. So I skedaddled." With a big obese grin on his face, Ken finished his story, quite proud of himself.

"You're jesting. You couldn't do such a dastardly deed at Christmas time," said a rather disconcerted Emil with a look of mild chagrin.

" – especially on Christmas Eve!"

"With the way all the stores jack up prices at this time of the year, I don't feel a bit guilty. All they want to do is give your pocketbook a drubbing. You know yourself, Emil, how you take a little extra cream off the top in your own business too."

"Sure do. That's because of brisk sales! But the only reason I would ever raise my prices is to make up for all the sticky-fingered shoplifters on the prowl at this time of the year such as yourself."

"Relax, Emil, it's Christmas. Can you believe it though," laughed Ken boisterously. "Can you imagine, me driving off with what looked like a whole green forest on the top of that cheap little red car?"

While Kenny and his wife Jeniffer were shaking with uncontrolled laughter, Emil and Ruth could only smirk with a very restrained chagrin.

Just then, Melanie reappeared at the door of the dining room. Once back in her chair, she gave herself to the business of eating with more spirit than before. A sense of Christmas jollity reigned over Melanie's demeanor and person while she sat quite pertly in her chair and ate so daintily, just like a little princess. Suddenly, the infectious Christmas spirit had captured little Melanie who seemed as cheerful as Christmas itself.

Melanie smiled so cheerfully and gaily to everyone at the table.

At once Ruth Wassel capitalized upon the welcomed change in her new daughter Melanie. "Hurry up and eat, Melanie, and we'll open the rest of the presents after dinner. There are some really big surprises for you, too, my dear."

"I can hardly wait," added Emil playfully.

Melanie smiled too at her Uncle Emil with a kind of bashful approval.

"I can't wait either," garbled Karen whose mouth was half full of after-dinner mints.

"Would you please eat your dinner, Karen, and leave those after-dinner mints alone," directed Jeniffer Winters rather impatiently to her daughter. "Then, perhaps, we'll open the gifts after dinner."

Such a homey celebration it was in the Wassels' dining room with a house full of cheer and a Christmas tree in the window that blinked laughingly through the atmosphere of this family feast. The variegated colors of the Christmas tree lights, shining red, yellow, blue, and green in the dining room front window, reflected merrily in Ruth's eyes as she cleared the table to bring forth the delicious deserts. The first dish was plump pumpkin pie crowned with clouds of whipped cream just as fluffy as Santa's beard. The second was hot mincemeat pie smelling juicy, sweet, and very tantalizing. After the servings were passed around according to the fetish of each one's appetite, everyone sated that last yearning for food which still remained. Iced creme-de-menthe for the adults and a glass of frosty cold milk for the children topped the feast with a feeling near bloat; hence, all attempts to stand up after this long repast could confound one's natural coordination. Thereafter the whole clan dispersed to the living room for the culmination of what was a perfect Christmas Eve.

The first to enter the living room was, of course, Emil who entertained a certain sense of Christmas megalomania and thus had to supervise virtually every Yuletide activity that he could, however large or small it might be.

For no apparent reason, Emil froze in the middle of the living room and stared and stared at the Christmas tree as if someone had literally torn out his very heart and soul. All the faces of the other Christmas revelers aped Emil's disconsolate expression, too, because of their identical expressions of shock. The prevailing mood was one of someone ambushing the whole Christmas adventure, for every gift which was beneath the colorful tree had been recklessly scattered towards the center of the living room, far from the proper place of reverence. Nothing could have more provoked Emil Wassel to a state of perturbed ire than such a sacrilegious swipe at Christmas.

"Look at this mess. What has happened here? Who could have done this? How could anyone do such a thing to Christmas? What's that dollhouse doing underneath the Christmas tree?" shouted an agitated Emil Wassel in a state of utter exasperation.

"I don't believe it, either,"quipped Ken who was rather bewildered.

"Aren't we going to have any Christmas, daddy?" asked a disappointed Karen.

"How horrible!" added Jeniffer with indignant surprise.

"Why I've never seen anything quite like this before at Christmas time," said Ruth with sheer disbelief.

"Where's Melanie?" blasted Emil with a bellicose authority to his voice.

Everybody searched for Melanie, but she had vanished in the direction of her bedroom at the first sign of controversy. By now, Emil, who was thoroughly perplexed by the whole affair, noticed a peculiarly cold feeling creeping over him. It was inescapable, for everyone around the room could sense it too, including his wife Ruth who could perceive virtually everything in her husband after being married to him for forty-one years: unmistakably, it was the onset of the seasonal malady known as the Christmas blahs.

"That dollhouse," bellowed Emil in a frustrated daze. "Look what that dollhouse has done to our Christmas. How could she do such a thing to us after we gave her that doll? She's got to be punished for this," resolved Emil firmly.

This twist in his plans made Emil feel extremely nervous because everything had to go just perfect for him at Christmas time, but a disaster unprecedented was upon him, quite unlike any he had ever experienced before in his entire life.

"Wait a minute, Emil. Wait!" remonstrated Ruth so plaintively.

Emil was already turning towards the back hallway leading to Melanie's bedroom. However, Ruth pulled at his arm firmly to thwart his progress, for Ruth wanted to diffuse this ugly scene as quickly as possible, moreover, she realized this incident would have the same affect as an ice-storm during a Christmas parade to stop Christmas revelers from all their jubilance.

"Melanie's simply not been herself lately. You know it. Calm down, now dear! Just put the presents back under the tree."

Swiveling around, Emil reluctantly heeded Ruth's advice and swung his huge trunk over to pick up the gifts that Melanie had scattered about the living floor. With haste he stacked the gifts in piles and then returned them all to their former positions of esteem beneath the Christmas tree.

All the expensively and richly decorated packages in their silvery red, white, and green boughs were once again studied as these Christmas revelers stared at the gifts and each other in stark wonderment while Emil Wassel completed his work.

Still the dollhouse stood majestically beneath the center of the Christmas tree and peeked over the multitude of gifts with a loftiness all its own; nevertheless, it was barely visible above the stacks of gifts except for the second story, roof, and chimney. The world within Melanie's dollhouse was sealed off completely because the opened front door had been tightly closed in the nervous rush by Emil to clean up the mess. Nevertheless, the foreground of presents, decorated in garish colors of silver and gold and glorious Christmas designs of snowflakes, winter scenes, and evergreens accentuated the utter simplicity of the little bright blue dollhouse with its gabled white trim roof, and matching columns. There was, however, a beautiful angelic spirit hovering over Melanie's dollhouse, and it had lit upon the top of the chimney to remain. The angel was dressed in virtually the same garb as the baby blue doll which Melanie had received for Christmas. This celestial spirit was entering the dollhouse from above, as though it were attempting to climb down the chimney.

Thereupon the Winters and the Wassels proceeded with their festive ritual of gift-giving. With loving care, Emil pulled the packages, one-by-one, from beneath the tree and distributed them amongst their cheerful and enthusiastic recipients who were now scattered around the living room again in their favorite easy chairs. A semblance of jolliness once more charmed this Yuletide gathering, but the exuberance demonstrated at this height of cheerfulness was most apparent in the littlest of its members.

"What do you have for me, Uncle Emil?" questioned Karen with excited little-girl anticipation.

"What do you think of this, sweetheart?" offered Emil. He held a lengthy gift wrapped in bright red tissue paper in his outstretched hand which he held right before her.

" Is that really for me, Uncle Emil?" begged Karen.

"You bet, my dear. From Aunt Ruthie and me," smiled Emil with warmth to his little niece.

With unrestrained curiosity, Karen stripped the long package of its wrappings and brandished a candy cane in the air that was nearly as big as her plump self. In fact, she quickly pulled off the cellophane wrapping and was licking the sweet treat with unbridled palatal pleasure. "Wow! Where'd you get this candy cane, Uncle Emil?" queried little Karen.

"That's a secret that only Santa Claus knows," smiled Emil happily.

As rapidly as Emil distributed the gifts, so were they being opened. Ruth had lifted the top from a rather large oblong box only to discover a floor length coat made from elegant beaver.

Within seconds Ruth Wassel had filled the dark gray woolen coat with her entire self and was bouncing around the room like a veritable model. She twirled around and around in circles, showing off her Christmas spoils.

"What a darling coat, Jeniffer. It must have cost you a small fortune. Why I'll be embarrassed when you open our gifts after this," observed Ruth Wassel.

"Oh hush up, Ruthie! You look like the coat was made especially for you and nobody else." chuckled Jeniffer with jollity.

"And do I ever agree," offered Ken. "You look so sharp, my dear!"

During Ruth's exclamations of praise for the fur coat, Kenny was ripping some silvery green paper and a matching bow from a tiny box that was nearly hidden in his big fleshy palm. While he was removing the remaining tissue from the tiny box, a feverish curiosity scintillated over the faces of all the onlookers, no less resplendent than the shining Christmas tree lights of red, blue, green, and orange reflecting about the room.

"We couldn't afford that much this year, Kenny," observed Ruth with a grin, "so we hope you will understand."

Kenny caught the glimmer of humor in Ruth's eyes and just smiled smugly to himself and said: "Just so you two didn't afford any less than we did – you're all right," laughed Kenny.

Everyone echoed the merry laughter of Ken Winters as the whole living room shared the fresh joy of his holiday cheer.

Ken then went about the pleasantries of opening his gift as delicately as his big hands would allow. Suddenly, the secrecy of his endeavors was disclosed. Kenny gracefully slipped over his left hand a diamond wrist watch in gold with matching expansion band, the crystal of which had tiny diamonds set all around the sparkling face, and they glittered each time Kenny moved his wrist in the colorful red, green, and blue from the nearby Christmas tree shining upon it.

"Just what I've always wanted, a beautiful wrist watch--and a gold one at that. And what attractive sparkling jewels around the face!" boasted Ken Winters. "Sure hope I don't lose it like most of the watches I've owned." observed Kenny casually.

"He sure won't lose this one," stated Jeniffer Winters authoritatively.

"Look what I've got, Ruthie," announced Emil proudly.

"What is it?" said Ruth excitedly.

Emil wrestled with a box of gigantic proportions for some time before he freed a winter coat that looked more like a blanket than anything else, simply because the living room was almost covered by it. Emil swung the woolen brown coat around his shoulders and it hugged him all the way down to his knees. Then he buttoned the thick coat down the front, buckled a very wide belt around his rotund middle section, and finally pulled the hood trimmed in brown fur up around his head. He smiled with glee and shouted to all the company.

"Ho! Ho! Ho! Merry Christmas." laughed Emil as his bulbous red cheeks rejoiced.

Emil's antics decked everyone's face in a jolly grin. The room echoed with a belly laugh as Emil went through his gyrations of cheer.

"Now there's no chance you'll ever be cold again at Christmas time." glowed Jeniffer with mirth.

The festivities of exchanging gifts proceeded throughout the evening for nearly an hour as Emil unpiled gift after gift from beneath both trees in the living room and dining room. An empty box served as a makeshift wastebasket that soon became stuffed to overflowing with crumpled gift wrapping and the torn ribbons and bows. Beside each one of the Christmas revelers was a pile of gifts the likes of which any Christmas tree could boast.

"Look at what I just found!" announced Emil with a note of surprise. "On a fir branch towards the back of the tree. I must have not been paying attention to this little surprise. I wondered where it came from." Emil was just about to reach for another Christmas present when he noticed this little surprise.

"Did you see what I discovered, Ruthie? A little envelope. Here you open it, my dearest." It says: " Uncle Emil and Aunt Ruth on it." Emil at once put the little envelope in Ruth's outstretched hand as she sat in her rocker. Opening the card, Ruth looked somewhat befuddled and confused as she read the words written by a little hand: "Merry Christmas Aunt Ruthie and Uncle Emil, are we going to St. Anthony's for Christmas?" Melanie

"What do you believe Melanie means by this, Emil?" queried Ruth.

Jeniffer Winters looked up as she set her cup of rum aside on the nearby end table next to her arm chair and said; "Isn't that where you attend Church?".

"Why, yes," said Ruth Wassel. "But that was years ago."

"You mean you gave up church attendance like we did? Sundays are simply not my day," responded Ken Winters. "I drive my rig six days a week and get only one day off and I have to have my sleep."

"Exactly!" confirmed Emil. "Six days a week I'm in the toy shop. I have to have my rest on the seventh day."

"You bet," asserted Ken Winters. "After all, isn't it the day of rest?" offered Ken rather humorously.

Everyone kind of laughed at Ken's humorous outburst.

"Well, she must want to go to church, don't you think Emil?" queried Jeniffer. "You know how seriously Teddy and Chrissy took their faith."

"I suppose we might have Mrs. Apple, next door, take her to church for Christmas. After all she's a sweet old lady and Irish Catholic and an avid church goer," offered Emil.

"I'm not giving up my day of rest and Christmas is on Sunday this year," boasted Ken.

"That includes me, too," responded Emil in assent.

"Let me tell you, Kenny, Mama Claus will make sure you are out of bed tomorrow, bright and early, just as she did last year for Christmas Mass. You can be sure there will be no wintertime naps on Christmas morning!" boasted Jeniffer Winters. "If there is one day a year you will go to Church it will be on Christmas."

"All right, dear," returned a somewhat muted Ken Winters.

"Now it's time we continue with the Christmas party before Santa arrives," returned Emil. "or we'll spoil it all for Karen and Melanie! Look and see what I just found under the Christmas tree; without a doubt it's the tiniest of all the presents."

It was towards the end of the Christmas party that eyelids widened and focused upon this tiniest Christmas present of them all. Jeniffer cradled a delicate package protectively in her hands because she was so obsessed with its fascinating appearance. The elaborate green bow and the golden wrapping paper gave this little box an enviable affluence in spite of its size. Beneath the richly wrapped paper and the lid of the box, Jeniffer found an ornate golden ring. A Christmas tree of diamonds shone from the setting of the ring as she slipped it onto her right ring finger. Jeniffer then passed her hand from right to left in the light as she so proudly displayed her diamond ring at full arm's length. The reflections emanating from the tiny diamonds on Jeniffer's ring were the same splendorous colors of the twinkling Christmas tree ornaments nearby.

"Just what I've always wanted!" chuckled Jeniffer Winters who couldn't stop admiring this most beautiful Christmas gift. "I simply adore the way the ring reflects the lights of the Christmas tree ornaments. The diamonds literally take on the different colors of the tree. I am so touched by this gift, Emil and Ruthie. It must have taken you ages to find this ring in the department stores. I am so thrilled by this present. I don't know what to say! Thank you. Thank you, Emil and Ruthie."

"Truly, I spent more time searching for just the right gift for you, Jeniffer, than I did on all the rest of the gifts together." explained Ruth. "I went from jeweler to jeweler and from shopping center to shopping center and from store to store. I really hope it's just the right size for you, dear."

"Without a doubt, Ruthie, it fits absolutely perfect. Why it's the most expensive looking ring I ever saw. Santa Claus might have not emptied his bag completely into your own stocking, yet Ruthie. I'll wager he left something over at our house for you. Just you wait and see, Ruthie."

Once everyone had settled down into their seats and all the gifts had been eyed over and over by the recipients, a distant melody aroused these Christmas revelers. This soft soothing music enkindled the curiosity of all those present so much that they jumped from their chairs and congregated in haste around the front door of the Wassels' home. Most everyone believed a choir of carolers had assembled outside to sing a song or two in the neighborhood so that the holiday spirit would spread abroad. Without delay Emil swung open the front door and on the steps before him he saw three youths around twelve years of age who were all bundled up in brown leather jackets, red stocking caps, and white scarves. Their stocking hats and coats were bespeckled with a conglomeration of snowflakes that had accumulated into little white clusters of fluff against their winter outfits. As soon as Emil Wassel had opened the front door, a gust of frigid December air and blowing snow came rollicking past the threshold like children rushing through the school door for Christmas vacation.   Suddenly, all the cute little reindeer candles in the vestibule windowsills and on the little decorative tables on each side of the front door were extinguished from the arctic gust of wind blowing through the door. As cold as it was with the door opened, the Wassels and the Winters quickly forgot their discomfort because a warmth of a different sort began to heat their bodies.

The Yuletide orchestration of the boys' voices had so penetrated the quarters of the Wassels' living room that both families wanted to sing along with the lads because their hearts had been rallied by the boys' excited voices. When they attempted, however, to mouth the words of

"Silent Night, Holy Night" with the carolers, all that came forth was a garbled disharmony of discordant notes. The coldness of the evening and the falling snow prompted the boys to carol forth the words of this Christmas favorite so rapidly that barely anyone could keep up with them yet alone recognize the melody of this great Christmas favorite. Throughout the course of their caroling each boy eagerly held his gloved left hand out before him. In their right hands was a simple candle stub aflame, except for the youngest of the three boys, just ten years of age, whose candle had been extinguished by the gust of wind created by Emil opening the front door with such alacrity. Emil immediately understood the significance of this gesture, for he dug into his pocket for a gift and, in an instant, unfolded from his money clip a crisp new five-dollar bill for each boy.

Nor did Ruth Wassel hesitate to help the boy whose candle had blown out. "Here, young man, an extra little gift for you to see your way. It's quite difficult keeping one's candle lit on such a cold wintry night, so here's a miniature flashlight they're making nowadays for just such a predicament as yours. It will help you find your way back home before something bad happens to you on such a dark snowy night."

In a flash upon receiving their gifts, the boys whirled around and vacated the snow-covered front porch, leaving behind them only the trails of their vaporous breaths and their footprints in the falling snow. A mischievous giggle echoed through the stillness of the night as they vanished down the snow-piled street to the next house.

Without delay, Emil closed the front door and returned with the others to the welcomed coziness of the living room where the fire was gently burning into heaps of glowing embers. On the way, Ruth Wassel nudged Emil with her elbow.

"Didn't you recognize those boys, Emil? They sang carols here yesterday, and you gave them money then."

"Did I?" wondered Emil aloud.

"Yes, you did, my dear. And I'm sure they're from that one family down the street that has all those kids. You know the Smiths; I think that's their name. He's a school janitor and I don't believe he makes very much money."

"Why that's disgusting. To think that someone would sing Christmas carols for money," complained Jeniffer. "No Pointer's children would do that."

"I really felt kind of sorry for them," commented Ruth. Still I'm mortified seeing children out, wandering the streets like tramps on Christmas Eve, all alone."

"It's sacrilegious. That's what it is. Taking advantage of people's charity like that at Christmas," stated Ken Winters with disgust.

"They're only kids and maybe that's all they'll get for Christmas." countered Emil with an air of self-defense. "After all, what's Christmas without a gift?"

During the caroling Karen had helped herself to the dish of chocolates laid out for the company in between her trips to the front door to watch the carolers. Her face, therefore, was smeared with a chocolaty mess and her fingers were gooey and sticky like a taffy-puller's.

"Karen, look at the mess you've made of yourself," reprimanded her mother Jeniffer. She asked her husband Ken for a handkerchief and then began to clean away the sticky chocolate from her daughter's face and fingers.

"We had better start for home now, Kenny" suggested Jeniffer. It's kind of late and Karen has to go to bed and ten o'clock is already well past her bedtime." clarified Jeniffer.

With that everyone rose again from their living room chairs and began to mingle together for the end of what they thought was a perfect Christmas Eve celebration while they gathered their wraps and gifts together for their exit. The Winters prepared to depart with the cheeriest farewell that the Wassels could summon.

"Merry Christmas, Jeniffer," said Emil as he helped her into her coat.

"Merry Christmas, Kenny and Karen," said Ruth most graciously.

"Be sure to stop by tomorrow so we can get together at our place," suggested Jeniffer Winters. "I know we have a couple of gifts under our tree for you that I believe Santa forgot. After this wonderful evening, we would like to express our appreciation by inviting you over for Christmas dinner. Am I wrong or am I right, Kenny?"

"You're absolutely correct, my dear." affirmed Ken Winters. "I can almost taste your delicious apple pipe, piping hot, right now. As a matter of fact, my imagination can smell it clearly. Ken Winters was masticating with his mouth in between his words in humorous anticipation.

"We'll all be there-bright and early too," confirmed Emil happily. It's not our custom to turn down such generous invitations to dinner."

What do you think, Ruthie?" queried Ken.

"Affirmative. Affirmative!" smiled Ruth approvingly.

"If you're not there," announced Ken. "You can count on some big chunks of coal in your stockings this Christmas morning," laughed Ken. His antics caused everyone to chuckle merrily to one another in a kind of jovial culmination of all the Christmas festivities that occurred this Christmas Eve.

"Are you going to bring Melanie with you?" inquired Karen who was hugging her Santa Claus doll close to her chest. She was all bundled up in a brown woolen overcoat, knitted scarf and stocking cap of identical cranberry hue. She appeared quite prepared to face the harsh elements of a frigid snowy Christmas Eve.

"We sure are going to bring our dear Melanie along," stated Ruth with unequivocal certitude. "Christmas was just too much for her this year with all the excitement and I am certain she was overtired and has already fallen asleep in her room." Ruth gently patted Karen on the back a few times, as she spoke to assure her little niece of the veracity of her words.

With Karen all wrapped up in a winter wonderland of comfort and hugging her Santa doll close, she waved good-bye with her right hand as best as she could to her Uncle Emil and her Aunt Ruthie.

Reluctantly, Emil opened the front door and a bluster of frigid Michigan air whipped through the room, causing everyone to stiffen their limbs in defense from the brittle evening cold. Without delay, Ken and Jeniffer Winters likewise protected in their furry-collared black overcoats from the bitter cold of a dark December evening bid the Wassels a final farewell. Ken and Jeniffer's arms were packed so full of gifts that it was extremely cumbersome for them to negotiate an exit. Before long, though, they outwitted their piles of Christmas packages and were on their merry way down the snow-covered steps with Karen tagging just behind them. Through the ankle-high drifts, the Winters struggled together as the snow was diminishing to a nighttime flurry with the colder temperatures of midnight approaching.

III. The Afterglow

Once the Winters had disappeared, Emil immediately closed the front door to seal off those arctic gusts of wind that were forming snow sculptures outside. After the front door was closed tight, Emil Wassel returned again to the living room with a deep breath of quasi-satisfaction as he looked around the room at the remains of what he thought was a rather satisfying Christmas feast. Emil decided to move toward his favorite rocker for a brief respite of relaxation before bedtime, especially after all the frenzied activity of this eventful Christmas Eve. But all of a sudden, the evening began to rush together before his mind as he looked up at the Christmas tree, across the living room from his rocker. Most of the presents had been opened, but there were a few which had not. This Christmas Eve was to be more special than any other he thought, but somehow it did not seem so. All the Christmas lights on the tree, suddenly, blurred into a distracting collage of electrical color while a feeling most uncanny overtook him.

Emil Wassel groped for an explanation to this dilemma, for ostensibly all had gone as well as he could have expected on a day so special and exciting. This was the one time of the year that Emil had looked forward to all year long with the same kind of frolicsome expectation as a child waiting to come downstairs on Christmas morning. Emil Wassel truly loved Christmas and everything about it. And he believed he perhaps loved it more than most folks. Still, though, everything simply did not seem just right and he was unable to understand just why.

Emil was even more perplexed with his wife's activities. She was moving about the living room in a flurry and clearing away the empty bowls of hors d'oeuvres and the dishes of Christmas candy that had been laid out, as though nothing at all was awry.

What really melted Emil Wassel's heart and left him with that bottomless feeling of the passing of Christmas was that Ruth could so casually remove the boxes full of decorous spent Christmas wrap, that shiny, colorful, party-like paper which had been ripped and torn apart by eager hands. Emil's soul suffered the unmistakable symptoms of the onset of the Christmas blahs, that emptiness of spirit and absence of cheer which inevitably follows the opening of the gifts on a hollow feast.

Somehow Emil suspected that his wife Ruth was subject to this same holiday malaise, even though she appeared to be as vivacious as ever. He simply did not want to ask her for fear she, too, was experiencing the same unmistakable symptoms of the Christmas blahs. Something was definitely awry but Emil was uncertain of what precisely the cause of it might be. How bare the base of the fir tree appeared to Emil now that all the gifts had been opened, except for that isolated few back by the dollhouse. Emil wanted so much to capture Christmas as totally his own and keep it with him all year long; however, this year it seemed as futile as having his new daughter Melanie understand Christmas.

While Ruth scurried about the living room to clean it up, Emil's mind, beset with the blahs, could only review the grim passing of Christmas. Emil rocked up and down and his chair perfectly syncopated itself to the rhythms of his nervous mind. The living room appeared to Emil as cold as he felt inwardly. Whenever he looked over at the dollhouse beneath the Christmas tree, or the thought of Melanie crossed his mind, he froze a little bit more.

Emil envied the snow flurries in the light of the outdoor Christmas decorations doing their sprightly dances through the cold breezes as though they had some secret of joy to be shared on Christmas Eve. Inside, though, a definite frigidity ruled over the Wassels' domicile. Having been neglected, the hearth was snoozing in a bed of nearly dormant coals; consequently, very little heat was being reflected to Emil and Ruth. How soon, mourned Emil, the Christmas trees would suffer a similar fate: be taken down and abandoned in a cold, cold abandoned alley. There was simply nothing more depressing than a dead Christmas tree lying all alone in a snowy alley.

Unable to cope with this frozen and cheerless atmosphere any longer, Emil rose from his rocker in order to take his pipe from the rack which set atop the mantel to enjoy an evening smoke. Certainly he could thaw out his frozen self with a bowl of his favorite tobacco blend and thus revive his sagging spirits. He tapped the spent ashes repeatedly from the pipe into his palm and discarded them into the fireplace and then repacked the bowl with his lusty cherry flavored tobacco. He mechanically reached for one of the long stick matches that had been placed on the mantel top for fires. On the underside of the projecting stone shelf top, he lit one of the matches, and with the help of several thoughtful puffs, set the bowl of fragrant tobacco afire. After extinguishing the match by waving it in the air, he flipped it into the remains of the burnt away Yule logs.

To further dispel these Christmas time blahs Emil seized the poker from the nearby rack of fireplace hardware. He pushed and poked at the smoldering remains until he succeeded in stirring up clouds of smoke and flying embers. Here and there, flames leaped forth as the fire broadcasted that poverty of warmth suitable for the addition of another log. He dumped on a hickory log of sizable proportions, hoping to gain from it the warmth and mellow fragrance he so much desired.

Such was not the case, however, for his fantasies of warmth were confounded as soon as he returned to his rocker and his pipe-puffing reveries. The blahs of Christmas would not cease their harassment of Emil Wassel. He saw his Christmas pride and joy drooping ever so sadly and perceptibly before his unbelieving eyes.

All the tinseled and electrical beauty of Emil's efforts had been frustrated by the sagging appearance of the Christmas tree with its seemingly misshapen branches. A dilemma of this sort, it so happens, was ordinarily quite elementary to Emil's Christmas tree expertise. Doting over the tragedy no longer, he exited to the kitchen to prepare the solution for this unfortunate occurrence.

In moments, Emil returned with a pitcher full of the medication that revives all such sick Christmas trees. First, he filled the tree stand in the dining room with the watery solution, then he entered the living room to do the same. Near the back of the evergreen, he squatted to the floor on his hands and knees to pour the curative solution of sugar and water in the evergreen stand while Ruth worked on the back side at her own

clean-up projects. Even though all the jolly mirth of old St. Nicholas had riotously burst forth shortly before that evening, these two Christmas revelers were, for a time, subdued by the hollow stillness overtaking their festively decorated home.

Having decided to interrupt her chores of clean-up after the Christmas party, Ruth departed for a time from her husband to check in a motherly way upon Melanie to see if she was all right. This she had done several times earlier during the Christmas party and after, at surreptitious moments when both the guests and her husband were unaware because she was particularly uneasy about this new daughter of hers and the way she was reacting to her new home. Things clearly seemed askew to Ruth Wassel and it was most difficult to put her finger exactly upon the cause of this dilemma. This time, as before when she checked, no light was peeking from beneath the doorway, only slightly ajar; hence, she still presumed her new daughter was yet sleeping. Nevertheless, if only to assure herself once more, Ruth so carefully opened the door

enough for only her head to see inside the bedroom and then she searched for the little Christmas doll who had fallen into disgrace. The widening crack in the doorway swept a larger beam of light across the bedroom floor, thus revealing the heavenly peace of a sleeping child. Accustomed to few luxuries, it was with little, therefore, that Melanie was at ease and so the floor where her dollhouse had rested became the most comfortable bed. Tearfully Ruth viewed a wrinkled handkerchief clinging loosely to Melanie's limp hand. Convinced of her new daughter's safety, Ruth elected to return to the living room after she covered her little angel with a warm blanket. However, it was only with great difficulty that Ruth composed herself and returned to the living room and the business of reorganizing things after the Christmas party.

Directly Ruth undertook another chore as she returned to the living room. She began to crawl around on all fours beneath the Christmas tree in search of those bits and pieces of paper wrapping that had been scattered pall-mall during the excitement of opening presents. So carefully, she collected these remnants of holiday cheer that one would believe she was going to put them all together again and solve the inscrutable puzzle of the passing of Christmas and the Christmas  blahs, which she herself felt too. Noticing the swirls of dried needles beneath the tree, she swept at them with her hand and said: "Emil, did you see all these needles on the floor here? What's happening to this Christmas tree?"

"I just don't understand, Ruthie, why the trees are so sick and I feel just as sick about it all myself." clarified Emil. "As a matter of fact, I feel more ill than the trees themselves. I have never experienced Christmas trees looking this miserable until this year, Ruthie."

"I thought these were going to be great trees when you brought them home from Fred's Filling Station." responded Ruth.

"So did I, darling," agreed Emil. "But if I had only remembered to put water in the tree stands, then this might not have happened. I hope this will heal them and we won't have any more problems with them. It's impossible to tell, though, because some trees are just plain desiccated, no matter what one does."

At this turn of things Emil drew a bigger than usual puff from his pipe, one of accomplishment, for things seemed to be approaching a state of normalcy with all the water properly emptied into the tree stands. After kneeling beneath the Christmas tree in the living room, Emil Wassel stood up with the empty pitcher of water as he took a couple of deep breaths to steady himself. He felt more assured since he had done all that he could; therefore, he hoped that all should be well.

"I'm glad you found what's wrong with the trees, Emil. But I want you to know that I'm still upset– terribly. I believe we really hurt Melanie and I don't know whether she's going to take to us. It's not that I don't want Melanie to be our daughter, Emil, because I want a daughter like Melanie more than anything else in this world. Suddenly, Ruth broke into tears, whimpering as she continued: "You know, Emil, how I've always wanted a daughter like Melanie. The trouble is that she was raised in such different circumstances than ours. You know how Teddy and Chrissy lived in the UP," Ruthie continued as she sat upon her knees next to Emil beneath the towering fir tree. "I hope I am wrong, but I just don't think she likes it here in the city with our style of living."

"Nonsense," returned Emil. "We had to punish her. We had no choice as good parents. At first, I thought the only reason why I have the Christmas blahs this year was Teddy and Chrissy's absence this Christmas. But I'm sure the way Melanie behaved this afternoon was what really set it off. To think she could be so naughty on Christmas Eve and undo all my hard work. I just can't believe that Teddy and Chrissy raised her to blaspheme Christmas and strip a Christmas tree of all its gifts. Why that's the very heart of Christmas!"

"Emil, she's only nine years old," sniffled Ruth. "And she doesn't even realize yet what a real Christmas is like."

"I know. I know." stated Emil with exasperation. He had put aside his empty pitcher of water on a nearby end table and was helping Ruth move the gifts aside to find those scraps of littered wrapping paper that she was so busy pursuing.

"I've got half a notion, though, to tell Santa to leave a hunk of coal in her stocking tonight instead of all those toys he planned to give her from his toy shop."

"Now listen to me, Emil. You cannot do that to her after all she's been through last Christmas," pleaded Ruth. Her brow was furrowed and her voice cracked with whimpering emotion when she sat up again from her work to address Emil. A pile of scrapped wrapping paper, including every Yuletide design and color imaginable, was forming on the floor before them.

As Ruth moved aside the opened gifts to reach for some more scraps, she caught sight of something that begged for her attention beneath the fir tree. A scrap of paper is a scrap of paper but, whatever this was, it wouldn't respond to her yank, for it was secured in position by the weight of the dollhouse resting upon its upper edge. Once she had freed what resembled a do-it-yourself Christmas note from beneath the weight of the dollhouse, Ruth could study her find with more leisure. This makeshift Christmas note was a folded over piece of cardboard with Christmas wrap taped to its reverse side. On the decorative side Ruth right away recognized the baby-faced winged seraphs floating their way across the decorative paper, for she had used it earlier to wrap Melanie's present. Puzzled as Ruth was, her eyes closely scanned the markings on the inside of the Christmas card. Holding it between her thumb and forefinger, she saw three little trees of Christmas green which had been simply shaped and crayoned across the card. There was a large tree, a medium sized tree, and a tiny tree. Ruth then turned her attention to the scribbled lettering on the Christmas note. Nothing could have been more beautiful for Ruth to behold than the seasonal color of red letters printed below by the little author's tiny hand. They spelled out the words: "Merry Christmas to my new mommy and daddy" in the uncoordinated hand of a child's writing.

Half wondering and half rejoicing the surprised Ruth at once waved the Christmas card before her husband who had now begun to assist her beneath the fir tree by sweeping together loose needles and paper scraps.

"Look what I've found," shouted Ruth Wassel. "It's just so-cute!"

Emil immediately stopped his crawling around the Christmas tree on his hands and knees and was perched upward in a kneeling position, resting his huge self on the heels of his shoes exactly like his plump wife.

"What is it? Let me see," begged Emil with a nervous curiosity. Studying the message in Ruth's outstretched hand, Emil too read the good tidings of Christmas joy printed in the bright red and green colors of the season. Emil puffed thoughtfully on his pipe over this incident and therewith folded his arms as was his custom whenever something important was troubling him.

"Can't you see? Can't you see, Emil?" asked Ruth rather tenaciously.

"Sure. It appears to be a note from Melanie," announced Emil with matter-of-fact conviction. "What's it supposed to mean?"

Emil's mutterings in between puffs of smoke only frustrated Ruth Wassel who had become thoroughly wrapped-up in the significance of her find. Ruth's cheeks turned to a poinsettia red as her eyes now flushed forth the grandest tears of joy.

"Emil, don't you realize what Melanie's given us for Christmas? Its her most treasured possession-her dollhouse." said Ruth with overflowing joy.

Piqued now with animated curiosity over the gift, Emil began to survey the premises of Melanie's little house with a more studious eye. Leaning forward on both his hands and knees, he opened the big front door of the Victorian home which hid the secret of Melanie's Christmas present.

Ruth, too, knelt forward so she would not miss any part of the surprise. Exposed before their wondering eyes was an empty dwelling save for three lonely figures in a virtually unfurnished living room on the first floor. In the center of this room, there was a single piece of furniture and nothing more. It was a small box filled with that white shredded paper used to package only the finest of Christmas gifts. In it lie the tiniest of the three dolls, a sleeping babe.

At first there was nothing extraordinary to Emil or Ruth about Melanie's

three wooden dolls, carved simply and dressed so modestly, for on numerous occasions they had seen Melanie playing with them for hours at a time. With serenity the mother doll looked over her sleeping babe while the father doll watched on protectively over them both in the hushed stillness of the little house. They all rested in such a placid peace beneath the guiding presence of the blue angel of Christmas above, dressed in identically the same attire of the doll Melanie had received from her Uncle Emil and Aunt Ruth for Christmas.

Lingering there for a minute, Emil and Ruth Wassel studied the dolls in silence. When they finally looked upward, rather meditatively in this serene silence, the little blue angel of Christmas warmed their hearts, revealing to them what Melanie had lost and found in Christmas. The bells of Christmas joy rang briskly through the Wassels' hearts, causing Emil and Ruth to see the true spirit of Christmas joy in their new daughter's heart.

"Emil! Emil!" said Ruth through a rush of joy and rain of tears. "Let me use your handkerchief, darling."

"Sure, Ruthie. Sure." replied Emil both despondently and obliviously. "Sure."

While staring into the dollhouse, Emil repeatedly used his index finger to wipe away the droplets of tears forming at the corners of his eyes. Finally, Emil brought himself to comply with Ruth's request. Once he passed the handkerchief to Ruth, she buried her reddened face in it, blew her nose gently several times, and simpered some more. All Ruth could utter through her melancholy was, "Emil, Emil, what have we done to this sweet innocent little girl, the joy of Therese and Terry's life?"

Emil wrapped his arm around his wife and gave her a gentle squeeze of comfort. "Now calm down, darling. You're making me all upset. It's Christmas and it's here to stay now that we have a new daughter."

"But we don't, Emil," whimpered Ruth. Once more, another fit of tears gushed forth from Ruth's already swollen red eyes, much to Emil's chagrin.

Emil then arose and proceeded to pace restlessly back and forth in the room, puffing on his pipe and wondering how to stop all those tears from falling down on Christmas Eve. Watching Ruth sniffle so was once again dampening Emil's jolly ways; consequently, he left the room in a dither. Ruth eventually pulled herself back together by completing her clean up chores before the tree. She finalized the house cleaning procedures by removing all the piles of scraps and the collected dried out needles which had fallen from the trees. The only remaining task was to replace the few Christmas gifts, scattered around the room, which she had moved in order to clean-up everything beneath the Christmas tree.

A frolicsome Emil bounded back into the living room with a bundle of joy in his arms, but there was some struggle because he was loaded down with his biggest and very best Christmas gift of them all.

Even Santa himself with his enormous sack of Christmas treasures could not have been prouder. Emil was so sure that this would definitely alter Ruth's sagging spirits and dispel once and for all the seasonal sickness of the Christmas blahs from his home. When his wife Ruth saw the package of joy Emil cuddled close to his heart in bear hug fashion, she halted in her steps and forgot all about her accomplishment of having just removed the last pile of scraps from beneath the Christmas tree. Emil wore a Christmas smile of good will that stretched across his face, the familiar smile one sees on the excited faces of gift-givers who are anticipating the joyous response of those they love. His cheeks glowed to a cranberry red with Christmas satisfaction as he sat down in his favorite rocker next to the Christmas tree and hearth while he cuddled his Christmas gift so closely.

"How do you like what I have for you for Christmas, darling Ruthie?" bubbled Emil. "A little Christmas doll."

"You always know what I want for Christmas, sweetheart. Where did you find this pretty little angel all dressed up in such bright Christmas red?" smiled a sniffling Ruth from her own rocker nearby.

"Oh, she dropped from a heavenly cloud into Santa's sleigh and was left for us last Christmas," laughed Emil.

With a mischievous grin, Emil winked playfully to both Ruth and Melanie. During their conversation, Melanie's eyes repeatedly blinked open and closed in a wake-up-in-the-morning response. Her expression was one of apprehension, but the apprehension seemed to diminish in the comfort of warm happiness she first detected in her new parents' voices. Ruth, who was now kneeling at the foot of the rocker, reached lovingly for her daughter's hand and held it tightly in her own. This metamorphosis in Ruth's expression from that of levity to sincerity caused Melanie Wassel to cringe somewhat with fear because she didn't know what this new mood in her aunt and uncle really meant.

"You're not going to spank me, are you? I didn't do anything wrong did I?" begged Melanie rather sheepishly. One of her hands was half clenched in defense before her mouth, and her eyes peered with a disarming trepidation over it all.

"Oh no, Melanie. Oh no," pleaded Ruth with a reassuring smile of the deepest sincerity.

"We want to apologize to you," explained Emil, "for one big, big mistake on our part. We never, never made such a mess of Christmas before. I hope you'll forgive us because it's the biggest mistake parents could ever make," continued Emil.

"There's no better gift for Christmas than what you gave us, sweetheart." offered Ruth with a pat on her head.

"Why that's what Christmas is really all about, Melanie. It's the true spirit of Christmas," affirmed Emil. He had his arm around Melanie and since she was more at ease, the beginnings of a smile, therefore, blossomed on her little face.

"This has to be the very best Christmas we've ever had," smiled Ruth happily.

"And we'll never be without your dollhouse again at Christmas time," confirmed Emil reassuringly. "It's truly the very best Christmas Dollhouse – above all others."

"No one's Christmas gathering should be without one, sweetheart." finalized Ruth with the happiest Christmas smile.

With that Melanie reached upward and put her little arms around her new father's neck and gave him a big Christmas kiss on the cheek, in spite of his white stubbily beard.

"And I have a new mommy and daddy now for Christmas too." boasted Melanie.

"By all means and we have a new daughter too," said Ruth joyously.

"Will you both still be my aunt and uncle?" begged Melanie anxiously.

"We most certainly will." affirmed both Emil and Ruth.

"And look at daddy, how he's growing a white beard just like Father Christmas!" laughed Melanie quite merrily.

"What a surprise, I didn't notice, Melanie." observed Ruth with a giggle.

"Yes, you're right, Melanie. I am," chuckled Emil as he stroked the very beginnings of a beard. "I must have forgotten to shave!"

"Oh no, daddy, it's another miracle! Don't you see?" explained Melanie with eagerness.

"Why I'm so happy I could dance a jig!" boasted Emil with a grin. And Emil could not resist either because, for a quick minute or two, he danced little Melanie in a couple of festive circles, back and forth, around the Christmas tree and her dollhouse while holding Melanie's hands high in the air. Even Ruth, Melanie's happy new mother, merrily joined these two Christmas revelers herself.

Afterwards, both Emil and Ruth– panting and puffing– touched Melanie's cheeks from opposite sides with a kiss and everyone hugged each other simultaneously in a wreath of family love around the rocker and Christmas tree. The hearth too had sensed the warmth of Christmas in the Wassels' hearts; for it burned vigorously until the logs sizzled, crackled, and sputtered their sparks upward through the chimney till they joined the starry

night above. Even the Christmas tree shared in the festivities with its branches bouncing back again to their fresh evergreen flavor.

The cheer and joy of the season fused into one spirit when the Wassels made the last minute preparations for Christmas morning before bedtime. In front of the blazing hearth Emil, Ruth, and Melanie Wassel rearranged Christmas around the dominating presence of Melanie's dollhouse thus giving attention to all the wondrous gifts which they had received that Christmas. Having returned all the presents to their proper positions beneath the sparkling red, green, and blue colors of the fir tree, the Wassels were ready to hang Melanie's stocking on the fireplace in expectation of Santa Claus' arrival. All decked out in her velvety cranberry red Christmas dress; Melanie rejoined her mother and father at the fireplace. Emil assisted Melanie in tacking her stocking to the front of the mantel while Ruth stood by enjoying the intimacy of the whole affair.

"Be careful now, Emil, and don't miss the nail and hit Melanie's little fingers," admonished Ruth "Remember it's the first time you've hung a Christmas stocking in some time, sweetheart."

"Don't worry, darling. I may be getting older, but I'm an expert at Christmas with Melanie at my side," grinned Emil.

"It's such a joy to be together like this!" observed Ruth.

Emil's swing of the hammer rung true and Melanie's stocking was firmly in place before the hearth. A smile no smaller than the Christmas wreath on the Wassels' front door danced across Melanie's features and throughout the whole Wassel home with the closing of the day's excitement. From the stars at the top of the tree to the dollhouse at its very bottom the Wassels rejoiced together over all the treasures they had received that Christmas.

"There's just one thing we have forgotten," affirmed Emil as he unplugged the Christmas tree for the evening. "Let's make this a perfect Christmas this year. In order to do that we must take out our coats, hats, goulashes and gloves so we can attend midnight Mass to truly celebrate Christmas the way it is supposed to be. By the way, how long will it take for you two to spruce yourselves up for the trip to Church, Ruthie?"

"Oh, just a few minutes. It won't take us very long, will it Melanie?" replied Ruth with a merry tone to her voice.

"Oh no." returned Melanie with a new full expression of happiness to her face. "We'll hurry. I promise."

"Wonderful!" exclaimed Emil with a gentle Christmas smile. "It's been so long since your Aunt Ruthie and I have been to Church or midnight Mass for that matter. What a welcomed joy it will be, especially to be going to Mass with you, Melanie, our little Christmas doll. And you can open all your gifts Christmas morning, Melanie, right after Midnight Mass. All the presents from us and Uncle Ken and Aunt Jeniffer." said Emil with a look of such gentle assurance.

In but a few minutes Emil and Ruth Wassel and Melanie, accoutered in their wintertime overcoats, stocking caps, scarves, goulashes and gloves were through the front door of their own Christmas dollhouse and were wending their way down the snow-covered street towards St. Anthony's. In the distance, they could hear the Church's bells ringing out the Christmas carol, "Hark the herald angels sing, glory to the New Born King."

Merry Christmas to all and to all a Good Night!

Beautiful Assumption Grotto